12 Steps For Courageous Leadership

Start your Journey now!

Michael W. Kublin

with Jan Mayer-Rodriguez

authorHOUSE®

AuthorHouse™
1663 Liberty Drive
Bloomington, IN 47403
www.authorhouse.com
Phone: 1-800-839-8640

First published by AuthorHouse 06/06/2011

ISBN: 978-1-4567-1937-1 (sc)
ISBN: 978-1-4567-1938-8 (e)

Library of Congress Control Number: 2010919032

Printed in the United States of America

Table of Contents

Dedications

- Dedicated to my parents Al and Phyllis Kublin who live courageously every day. Mike

- Thank you to Margaret, Jacquelyn and Harrison who give me the ability and opportunity to live courageously every day. Mike

- To my sister Debra Faye Tritsch who is doing everything in her power to live courageously. Mike

- Dedicated to my parents, Nick and Betty Mayer, who lived their lives with courage and conviction; to my husband, Miguel Rodriguez who shares my beliefs, and to my daughters, Alex and Leah Rodriguez who are well on their way to living their lives with courage! Jan

- Dedicated to fellow leaders who continually learn, grow, and expand their knowledge, experience, and passion for life and help others do the same. Mike and Jan

- A special "thank-you" to Paula Santonocito for making this book a reality. Paula shared her expertise without hesitation and provided recommendations and encouragement along our journey. Mike and Jan

Introduction

Being a leader is not easy. It takes a real demonstration of living courageously. After observing many leaders who have come through PeopleTek programs, I noticed that the ones who are successful both in life and work have a set of characteristics and behaviors.

"I saw a pattern so clearly in these characteristics, I created a term to describe them and call it "CourageAbility"™.

CourageAbility is the ability to live both your dreams and professional life the way you want, while achieving your goals and exceeding in your life's ambitions and objectives. It is taking and empowering yourself and others to go where you or they have never gone before.

For the past 22 years I've been on a quest to be a great leader. Working with businesses and teams, and observing as a consultant, coach, trainer, and leader, I experienced both great achievements and disappointments.

PeopleTek's Leadership Journey has graduated over 1500 leaders from a wide variety of companies. Together with Jan and with PeopleTek coaches, I've had the opportunity to observe many leaders, styles, skills, traits and actions and have come to a conclusion: Courage is the single most important attribute any leader must have in order to be effective and successful.

We all have the ability to demonstrate courage and we need to master the skill to activate it "on command". As a result we have coined the term CourageAbility as a tool and trigger for all of us to use to remind us of the actions we can take to make vast improvements as leaders.

Courage is also required for choosing and developing our career whether in the corporate world, in private business, a public sector, or as an entrepreneur. This decision is solely ours and ours alone. As individuals we must take ownership for making the important decisions that impact our lives, our happiness, and our future.

Owning our career builds our leadership skills and enables us to become strong leaders for any team or any organization we lead or are a part of. And, by working on the CourageAbility factors, we can transform and strengthen leadership around the world one person at a time.

Please share with us your feedback, stories and responses to your use of CourageAbility and its practice in your quest to be a great leader. Enjoy your Journey!

Mike

Author's Note

With all my experience, study, and achievements, it wasn't until recently that I was able to improve my skills as a leader a small amount. In 1988 I was told that I was "wishy-washy", unfocused, and didn't hold my staff accountable to behavior.

While this hurt, through various coaches and self discovery I was able to learn where these perceptions were coming from and made many adjustments to my style and skills. Despite the opportunity to develop many successful teams, including PeopleTek, it was not enough.

It is only recently where I've noticed improvement in my leadership skills and I credit a majority of that change as a result of my experience with a network marketing business. Before this experience I felt I was lacking something in my behavior and confidence level. I can now impart a set of techniques that have been proven to be not only effective when practiced but enduring and everlasting.

Many of you may have cringed at the title *12 Steps For Courageous Leadership*. You may have even associated it with another 12 step program, Alcoholics Anonymous. Well yes, it is a term related to using 12 steps, and yes, I am taking a chance that everyone won't like me or it because of it.

I am proud to say with confidence "I don't give a DAMN"! That is one demonstration of what CourageAbility is.

You don't have to have everyone like you. The ability to live your passion and business life the way you want in order to achieve your career desires, goals, and objectives takes courage. While these 12 techniques seem simple and basic I can assure you they are easy to say and harder to do. With dedication and practice they can be implemented and your confidence as a leader will continually grow.

Sincerely,

Mike

Chapter 1

CourageAbility
What is it and how can it help us?

*"To succeed, one must possess an effective combination
of ability, ambition, courage, drive, hard work,
integrity, and loyalty." ~ Harry F. Banks*

It's not easy being a leader. It takes courage and commitment, the willingness to step out of our comfort zone, the need to readily adapt to change, and the obligation to develop our skill set and the skills within our organization.

To some this is fearful. Dealing with the unknown or facing a known weakness creates discomfort. Another way to look at it is that courage and commitment are required to become a stronger leader. Embracing both the fear and courage emotions we feel can actually be inspirational!

We have identified 12 areas that can de-rail our ability to be successful. This can be due to fear, or lacking the courage to:

1.   Passion~ Have and live your dream.

2. Document your goals.
3. Commit to your goals.
4. Understand your strengths and the strengths of others.
5. Communicate with confidence and clarity.
6. Understand and manage conflict with a purpose.
7. Develop others.
8. Delegate.
9. Develop a skill.
10. Remain controlled.
11. Reward and recognize.
12. Succeed and learn from failure.

You may say we are missing an important one: risk taking. I've thought about this long and hard and if you have the courage and commitment to have and live your dream you will demonstrate enough risk for a lifetime.

While working with individuals I often ask a question with the intent to determine what they're passionate about: "If you could do anything you wanted in your career and life what would it be?" With the follow-up question "What are you willing to do to live that dream?"

Many of us would say we will do anything, work unlimited hours, and be willing to encounter failures to have our dream come true. Having the ability to identify our dream is the first step, this then needs to be followed with applying daily actions to achieve and live it.

This is not easy and requires you as a leader to take risks and maybe fail. You must get up, dust yourself off, and take more risks until your dream is realized. The real courage comes in taking the necessary actions to overcome the barriers you are faced with.

Whether leading in the corporate world, in private business, a public sector, or as an entrepreneur, we hope the 12 Steps For Courageous Leadership serve you well!

Chapter 2

CourageAbility Step 1 of 12
Courage to have and live your dream.

Why do you think this is problematic for some? To start with, not everyone allows themselves to envision or identify their dream. They conduct day to day activities, are almost on "automatic pilot", do what they need to do to be moderately successful, but don't take the time to reflect on what really makes them thrive and feel valuable.

Some individuals dream only small dreams afraid of dreaming "big". What if that dream comes true? Why not make it all it can be? Some let others tell them what their dream should be rather than creating their own. How can others know what you truly want? Only you understand and have unlimited vision to your dreams; don't let others squelch your enthusiasm (even if it's someone you respect and appreciate).

What is your dream? What would make you truly happy? What would it take to begin to make progress towards achieving this dream? Have you established steps and a timeline? Some dreams take decades to achieve. Be realistic and realize that nothing happens overnight and that obstacles are not unusual but certainly can be overcome.

I attended a conference and a very special person, Dr. Myles Monroe said, *"There are many in the cemetery who have not lived their dream".* He said some individuals *want to* but always have excuses or other things they are doing. We can choose today not to be one of those people and put out our dream and take steps towards living it.

Write down your dream, summon the courage to take action, and then take control! Do it now!

Chapter 3

CourageAbility Step 2 of 12
Courage to document your goals

"People who have goals achieve far more than those who don't, and those who have written goals achieve the most of all". ~Robert McGarvey

Forrest H. Patton, a motivational speaker and author of Force of Persuasion, provides the following about having goals:

> *"A study was made of alumni 10 years out of Harvard to find out how many were achieving their goals," explains Patton. "An astounding 83 percent had no goals at all. Fourteen percent had specific goals but they were not written down. Their average earnings were three times what those in the 83 percent group were earning. However, the three percent who had written goals were earning 10 times that of the 83 percent group."*

Why? Goals keep us moving forward. They help us focus and track progress towards what we'd like to achieve. No one knows why a written goal is more effective than one that's known and understood but not committed to paper. Some psychologists theorize that writing triggers important processes in the subconscious, which in turn inspires action towards achieving those written goals.

Remember, goals bring clarity and require action.

Think in terms of what, how and when and think SMART

S	pecific
M	easurable
A	chievable and actionable
R	ealistic
T	ime-bound

Start small. You may want to write down one or two goals you can accomplish this year, a few more in the five year range, and one to accomplish over your lifetime. Understand that goals can be changed or dropped – the idea is to keep on target with what you truly want to achieve and remember, they must be measurable and have a completion date. Happy goal setting!

Chapter 4

CourageAbility Step 3 of 12
Commit to your goals

*"Reality forms around your commitments. The
achievement of your goal is assured the moment
you commit yourself to it". ~ Max Steingart*

Here's a simple plan to get you started with your
commitment:

- ✔ Verify the goals you set are SMART (specific,
  measurable, achievable and actionable,
  realistic and with time frames)

- ✔ Remove fear; understand what's causing you
  discomfort, feel it, process it, and then face it
  head on

- ✔ Ensure the goals you set are YOURS; don't try
  to live someone else's dream

- ✔ Review progress weekly, if not daily. Don't
  beat yourself up if you're not on target; rather

determine other courses of action that may work better for you

✔ Don't judge anything you did as "wrong" if you missed your goal or target; change how you're addressing that goal

✔ Celebrate your successes! Even small milestones can be motivating; as you make progress towards achieving a goal do something for YOU

Did you know it's not uncommon to have a fear for achieving your goal? Some feel an uncertainty and lack the confidence to understand and embrace how their life/career may change. They'd rather resort back to their comfort level and the "known". Winners know they will feel discomfort and don't let it impact their behavior or detract from their objective.

Others have a fear of being viewed as a failure if they do not attain their goal and as a result resist being committed to a goal. While we all experience failure at times, those that make commitments feel the fear but do it anyway.

Still others listen to the "chatter" of others who may disagree with the goals that were set. This can sink us quicker than quicksand! Please don't let anyone else's dreams become yours. Their fears will feed into yours and you will quickly and willingly let go of what you desire most. We work with a lot of people who say their dream is to become rich only to let someone else tell them what they plan to do to get it won't work. How do they know?

What would it take for you to get excited and motivated to achieve your goals? Don't be ashamed of your reason to attain your goals as that will impact your commitment. Your goals could be a promotion, wealth beyond your wildest dreams, security for your family, etc.

Determine what you really want, make a plan, commit to it, and go for it!

Chapter 5

CourageAbility Step 4 of 12
Understanding your strengths and the strengths of others

"You need to find people that compliment your skills in the key positions within your company." ~ Michael Lake

Many of us know what our strengths are, know where we have opportunities to grow, and enjoy the feeling of being appreciated and adding value to our organization. Those who solicit regular feedback and validate their feelings become even more self aware and confident and can focus on maintaining their strengths and lessening their growth areas.

But what about your colleagues, team members, and subordinates? How aware are you of their strengths? Do you surround yourself and build your team based on filling voids or do you prefer to seek talent and behaviors similar to yours?

It takes courage to let others "take the wheel and drive";

we as leaders need to understand the strengths within our teams, take a step back, and let others do what they do best.

This means facing our fears and apprehensions, understanding we can't be everything to everyone, having a willingness to let go, and enabling others to excel. Letting go takes tremendous courage. We've done so many tasks for so many years (some came easy to us, others did not), did them because we felt we had to, and now have the opportunity to let others shine and leverage their strengths.

Most of us have completed leadership assessments (Myers-Briggs, DiSC, Team Dimensions, etc.) where our preferences are identified. It's amazing to see just how clear the preferred roles and associated strengths are for each individual.

How successful would your team be if everyone had the same strengths and similar weaknesses? Clue: Remember that overusing a strength may result in becoming a weakness, and that no style is right or wrong, good or bad.

Build a network, get connected to the key people in your organization who are critical to your mission and goals and ensure the team members also understand one another's strengths. Understanding individual and team strengths and linking them with goal achievement will lend itself to growing your bottom line.

Know the strength(s) of each of your team members and leverage them to inspire success at both the individual and team levels.

Chapter 6

CourageAbility Step 5 of 12
Communicate with confidence and clarity

"The single biggest problem in communication is the illusion that it has taken place." ~ George Bernard Shaw

Do you have a clear understanding of how your leader, customers, and shareholders wish to be communicated with? Do your staff and peers have a clear understanding of how YOU want to be communicated with? Does everyone know what is expected of them in terms of what should be communicated when?

Keys to being an effective communicator:

- ✔ Know that both over-communicating and under-communicating are problematic

- ✔ Provide timely and well intended feedback

- ✔ Be an active listener

- ✔ Pick the best channel of communication

Picking the right channel of communication is a key skill for all leaders. To do this well you have to understand the richness of the channel and the type of message best suited for that channel.

Channels of Communication (in order of richness)

Face to face. Why is this the richest? Think about tone of voice, posture, gestures, eye contact, and body position.

Telephone. What items do you retain here? Which do you lose?

Computer/email/instant messaging. These modes limit you to text sharing only. Some people try to use smiling faces, phrases in parentheses, italics, or bold type to denote their emotional perspective, but the message, or its importance may not be correctly understood.

Memos/letters. This is pretty much one size fits all - everyone on the distribution list gets the same message.

Bulletins/Facebook/Twitter/general reports. This is meant for the widest possible audience and you have no knowledge as to who read them.

Given this, all channels of communication serve a purpose dependent on what's being communicated. We recommend that you know your audience and the message, identify the intent, list the main points and then choose the channel of communication that is the best fit.

We also suggest anticipating questions and being prepared with responses. Some key questions to help you prepare include:

- ✔ What is going to happen?
- ✔ Why is it going to happen?

✔ How is it going to happen?

✔ When is it going to happen?

✔ Who is it going to impact and how?

✔ How will concerns be addressed?

Taking the time to choose your ideal communication channel and preparing for questions (and maybe even resistance) will allow you to deliver your message with clarity and confidence.

Chapter 7

CourageAbility Step 6 of 12
Understanding and managing conflict with a purpose

"Successful leaders manage conflict; they don't shy away from it or suppress it but see it as an engine of creativity and innovation…" ~ Ronald Heifetz and Marty Linsky

"Without conflict there is no leadership."
- - Tom Kurtz, Executive and Career Coach

While the *"Without conflict there is no leadership"* quote is controversial, we can assure you that levels of healthy conflict are very good. The best leaders are those that know they need to stretch others and help individuals and teams be the best they can be. Without healthy conflict this won't occur. In fact if you are not experiencing any conflict you may want to ask yourself "why".

At PeopleTek, we have recently observed some entrepreneurs and found that they are constantly asking others to "push the envelope". They know this is good for everyone, and although some individuals don't like it, strong leaders know they must take others where they've never gone before. Believe us, this will create conflict!

When many people hear the word "conflict" they think of negative situations. It may be, or in its simplest form, it may mean a disagreement or difference of opinion which can be inspirational and lend itself to creativity and growth. Problems arise when differences are not managed: ill feelings surface, morale diminishes, and productivity suffers.

Kenneth Thomas and Ralph Kilman indicate there are 5 modes in which conflict may be managed. Some styles sound like they may be "better" than others but in reality there is no right or wrong style and all five modes are useful when used in the appropriate situation.

The 5 Conflict Modes Are:

- ✔ Competing - This is a power oriented mode and is assertive and uncooperative; the individual pursues his or her own interest at the expense of the other person.

- ✔ Accommodating - This is the opposite of competing and is unassertive and cooperative. The accommodating person neglects their own concerns to satisfy the concerns of others.

- ✔ Avoiding - Avoiding is unassertive and uncooperative. The individual does not pursue their own concern or those of another person.

- ✔ Collaborating - This is the opposite of avoiding where the individual is both assertive and cooperative and works to satisfy all of the concerns of everyone.

✔ Compromising – This falls between competing and accommodating and is both assertive and cooperative, a mutually acceptable solution is reached, and both parties make concessions to resolve the issue.

WHEN TO LEVERAGE EACH STYLE

The COMPETING mode is most effective when quick, decisive action is required and for important issues that may be unpopular or are vital to the organization. Examples include discipline, cost cutting, legal requirements, and enforcing company rules and policies.

ACCOMMODATING is useful when preserving harmony is essential, for allowing others to learn from their mistakes (where the risk is minimal), when you realize you can learn from others and that their position is likely a better solution or that the issue is much more important to the other person than it is to you.

AVOIDING is useful when there are more pressing issues, when others are addressing the situation and don't require your intervention, when gathering more information is more important than having an immediate response, when you have no chance of satisfying your own concerns, and to let people cool down and reduce tension and then readdress the concern at a later time.

COLLABORATING is useful when there are important issues on both sides which may not be compromised, must be integrated into a solution, and when there is a need to work through hard feelings that are impacting interpersonal relationships.

COMPROMISING is useful when there are time constraints and solutions must be obtained quickly, when your issue is moderately important, when two opponents of equal power are strongly committed to differing goals but must reach a solution (ex. labor contracts), and as a back-up when collaboration or competition fails.

An effective leader:

- ✔ Stretches others and takes them where they wouldn't go without their guidance
- ✔ Is aware of their preferred conflict style but readily uses all styles
- ✔ Recognizes the conflict styles of others
- ✔ Understands effective conflict management and when and how to get engaged
- ✔ Assesses if they are over or under using a style and determines how that may be impacting their leadership skills and abilities

Take the time to review your preferred style(s), assess how incorporating the use of other styles could make you a stronger leader, and remember that by stretching yourself and your team, results will improve!

Chapter 8

CourageAbility Step 7 of 12
Grow and develop others

*"The growth and development of people is the highest
calling of leadership." ~ Harvey S. Firestone*

I have personally experienced a true need to grow and
develop others in my network marketing experience. The
entire system is set-up for individuals to be helped if they
want to be. Their sponsor's responsibility is to ensure they
are successful and thrive. If they do, then their up line is
handsomely rewarded. With few exceptions this is totally
opposite of a traditional organization where the boss is
managing and leading others, but not necessarily with the
intent to be more successful than they are.

In my recent experience in a multi level marketing (MLM)
venture, my sponsor called me regularly to follow-up and see
if I needed any help. He made sure I was using the proven
system that's worked in the past and will work again if
followed. In all my jobs and roles in my professional life, I've

never seen it so clearly communicated that you must develop others to be successful.

Most companies and organizations are going through times of change - is your staff prepared for what they may be facing? Do they have the skill set required to remain valuable and support a revised mission, and the vision and goals to ensure success?

True leaders help others be independent and successful beyond their wildest dreams. This is accomplished by coaching, developing and leading others to where they've never gone before and wouldn't go by themselves. And it means giving them the feedback, tools, and training opportunities they need to succeed (which may require individuals paying out of pocket).

The individuals closest to the customer are the ones we as leaders need to help the most. They are the ones that provide the most impact to the bottom line and also are closest to the processes and skills that are ineffective and realize it first.

If we coach and develop others properly we as leaders and managers can react quickly and without hesitation, support the true vision, and ultimately increase success.

Developmental items to consider include:

- ✔ Ongoing development planning (addressing both strengths and deficiencies)
- ✔ Timely and consistent feedback
- ✔ Regular one on one coaching (minimally monthly)
- ✔ Building organizational bench-strength
- ✔ Talent assessment
- ✔ Talent retention

✔ 360° feedback

✔ On the job training

✔ Effective delegation

✔ Cross training

✔ Leveraging "magic dust" (the strengths and likes of others)

✔ Setting stretch goals

✔ Mentorships

The true success of leadership is measured by our ability to help others be financially, physically, emotionally, and spiritually independent, and by providing them with the ability to do the same for others. How successful are you?

Chapter 9

CourageAbility Step 8 of 12
Effective delegation

*"Surround yourself with the best people you can find,
delegate authority, and don't interfere as long as the policy
you've decided upon is being carried out." ~ Ronald Reagan*

*"The first rule of management is delegation. Don't try and
do everything yourself because you can't." ~ Anthea Turner*

Delegation frees time and provides an opportunity to develop others. Sounds good doesn't it?

As leaders we frequently spend too much time doing the task ourselves; we are working in the business instead of on the business. As leaders we need to step back from the tactical work and spend more time on creating strategies and developing others.

There are numerous reasons for not delegating tasks and sharing responsibilities. The most common are not trusting that the job will get done to our satisfaction, discomfort with assigning a boring task, or feeling guilty that the workload will be too great.

Here are some tips to help:

- ✔ Plan your delegations; assess the strengths of your delegate, match the assignment accordingly and assign a due date.

- ✔ Provide clear and documented instructions; this prevents misunderstandings and if the task is new to your delegate, they can refer back to your instructions.

- ✔ The best delegators provide the "what and when", and leave the "how" to the individual which is more empowering and motivating.

- ✔ Assess how long the task would take you and build in extra time for your delegate and obtain buy-in that the deliverable date is realistic.

- ✔ Ensure your delegate has the appropriate resources they need to be successful. Inform staff, co-workers, business partners, etc of your delegated role.

- ✔ Follow-up and monitor the progress; you may be needed to add clarity to the task or be nothing more than a sounding board.

- ✔ Acknowledge the contributions of your delegate and provide constructive feedback for areas of growth.

Effective delegation will increase morale, build your talent pool and strengthen trust within your organization, ultimately growing results and improving your bottom line!

Chapter 10

CourageAbility Step 9 of 12
Develop a skill

"Today, many companies are reporting that their number one constraint on growth is the inability to hire workers with the necessary skills." ~ Bill Clinton

We've already talked about developing skills in others; now we'll discuss developing ourselves. If someone asked you what your greatest skill or trait was, how would you respond?

Here are some things to consider:

- ✔ What do you do that adds the greatest value?
- ✔ What is your "magic dust"?
- ✔ What differentiates you from your colleagues?
- ✔ How sharp are your technical skills?
- ✔ Do you hone your skills as change occurs?
- ✔ How do you contribute to making your team strong and whole?

✔ How do you strengthen business partner relationships?

✔ Are you a mentor or do you have a mentor?

✔ Do you know what motivates you?

✔ What type of task or assignment excites you?

✔ What type of task or assignment do you resist?

✔ What does your feedback tell you about becoming stronger?

We don't always take the necessary time to assess our skills and contributions. We may have been strong in our prior position, but are we doing all that we can to better enable us for career advancement?

Some think that development is the responsibility of their company. Why limit it to that? In today's economy we need to keep our skills sharp. After all, we were all initially hired based on our skill set; it's up to us to remain marketable and have a competitive edge. Invest in yourself. Know what makes you a key contributor and keep those skills strong; simultaneously identify two things that need strengthening and begin now!

Chapter 11

CourageAbility Step 10 of 12
Remain controlled

"Leadership is a matter of having people look at you and gain confidence, seeing how you react. If you're in control, they're in control." ~Tom Landry

Self control is important. The ability to manage our feelings instead of allowing our feelings to manage us is beneficial for everyone, especially so for leaders. It requires courage to look at our emotional responses and understand how we as leaders can improve our interactions and relationships with our staff, customers, and situations.

Having the ability to feel and then respond with purpose, while remaining composed, is what we strive for daily and during difficult situations. If a person lets us down and we are angry, we need to have the skill to respond appropriately rather than blowing up or raising our voice. We suggest reviewing and becoming knowledgeable with our emotions so we can use them to our advantage. This means being familiar with an entire spectrum of feelings including happiness, anger, sadness, loneliness, rejection, shame, peace, etc.

The more control and awareness we have the better leaders we can be now and in the future. An example may be when someone did something we didn't expect and we overreacted. Some of us have yelled and screamed which rarely serves us well and more often than not puts us in disfavor with those that witnessed it. Once the composure is "lost", the damage is done and may not be recovered from even when composure is restored.

We all have hot buttons and we all know individuals that seem to have a "gift" to light those buttons up. To excel in leadership we need to be in control of our emotions at all times. (It's certainly easier when times are calm and steady but may challenge us in difficult and turbulent/crisis situations).

Some common items that lend themselves to control issues include:

- ✔ Surprises
- ✔ Unexpected change
- ✔ Incorrect/incomplete information
- ✔ Insubordination
- ✔ Deadlines, date changes
- ✔ Lack of commitment, buy-in or urgency
- ✔ Lack of team effort

We first must understand our feelings and our desired but perhaps unhealthy responses, and then calmly think about what response would serve us better. This may require postponing a response, which is fine (rarely do we HAVE to have an immediate response). If regrouping is required, make an excuse that you must attend a meeting or make a call, take a break, or step away from the situation but commit to providing a response by "X" time. Example: within the hour, the next day, etc

If you don't have the ability to get away from the situation, drop a pencil and take your time picking it up and take some deep breaths, or take a phantom phone call. Both buy you a few minutes to regroup and regain the control you desire. Remaining calm under pressure is an appreciated leadership trait, especially during times of change. Select a technique to use to better enable you to always remain composed and in control.

Chapter 12

CourageAbility Step 11 of 12
Reward and recognize

"Start with good people, lay out the rules, communicate with your employees, motivate them and reward them. If you do all those things effectively, you can't miss". ~Lee Iacocca

We all want to be appreciated and recognized when we've done a good job. As a leader, we sometimes overlook this, or we may have good intentions but don't make it a priority and it drops to the bottom of our "to do" list. Issues regarding rewards include:

- ✔ Given too often
- ✔ Given on a limited basis
- ✔ Given inconsistently
- ✔ Not linked to vision, mission and goals
- ✔ Not wanting your staff to be more successful than you are (not a problem in Network Marketing organizations because as a leader you are rewarded based on their success).

Rewards can be given in a variety of modes and do not all need to be financial to be motivating to the contributor. Yes, they can be monetarily related, but given tight budgets recognition may also be provided via newsletters, townhalls, employee of the month certificates, cross training opportunities, delegation responsibilities, and simple verbal and written "thank-yous".

One complaint we've heard in the past is being recognized for minimal contributions. People know when they or a peer deserve to be recognized; if the effort is negligible the reward is hollow and not meaningful. We heard a story about someone being recognized as the key contributor for the month and they had no idea what they had done "special". This caused confusion and embarrassment when they were asked why they received the award. The intent is for the receiver of the reward to feel good about their contribution and appreciated for their efforts.

Another source of dissatisfaction is providing recognition inconsistently. We recommend establishing criteria and reviewing team accomplishments on a monthly basis, or minimally, quarterly. True accomplishments will easily be linked to your vision, mission or goals enabling you to clearly state why the recognition is deserved.

Remember to recognize all individuals or teams that have supported the effort; this may include rewarding others not under your span of control. A fairly regular complaint revolves around only one individual or team being recognized for supporting and completing a goal, yet several individuals/ teams were key contributors. This leads to ill feelings and resistance to wanting to work as a team again.

PeopleTek also suggests encouraging individuals to recognize each other at team meetings. This will assist you with being informed of contributions you may not have been aware of, and allow you to more formally reward efforts that meet your reward criteria.

Again, here is where I say the MLM industry has the process down pat. You reward based on results only and everyone in the business has the same opportunity as everyone else. I've been involved only a short time however I have the same potential as those making millions of dollars. Mini interim rewards are also provided which show advancement towards your target; these are in the form of letters from the president with pins provided to those on target.

Money is one thing; recognition is another. In an MLM, everyone is recognized on stage for the levels they have achieved, and this is powerful. They are recognized for real accomplishments where volume has been added to the bottom line and the reason for the recognition is clearly defined to everyone. Everyone in the organization has the exact same chance to replicate what was done before them.

I think all organizations should take a snap shot of this and adjust their compensation and reward plans to align with the growth and profitability of the company. Everyone in the company must have a chance to excel.

Chapter 13

CourageAbility Step 12 of 12
Succeed and learn from failure

*"You can't have any successes unless you
can accept failure." ~George Cukor*

The word "failure" raises blood pressure in some and motivates others. Why? No one likes to fail; simply stated it just does not feel good and we're trained to be successful. Yet without failures and issues we wouldn't be able to thrive and grow as quickly as we do.

If we care too much about what others think about our successes or failures we are living their dream and not ours. I've learned more than ever as part of a Network Marketing team that other people including our families will try and steal our dreams for us. While they love us and want to protect us they can't see what we see for ourselves and future. We don't ever want to be looked on as a failure especially by our family. We must let that go and keep learning and growing even if we are failing and struggling. Can you imagine what would have happened if we didn't get up after falling when learning to walk or continually waited for the approval of our family to walk? We would never have moved. I encourage you to not want to be liked or supported by everyone. This was my biggest strength and hurdle as a leader. I can tell you that it prevented every aspect of my life from thriving with passion until it was recognized and dealt with.

For those of you involved with making or implementing any type of change in your profession do you track your success rate? When issues exist, do you conduct an analysis of what went awry? Even when successes have been experienced there's almost always opportunity to be even stronger. While conducting your post review of changes:

- ✔ Think out of the box
- ✔ Take time to reflect what could be done differently to inspire success
- ✔ LISTEN. What are you hearing and feeling?

Chapter 14

CourageAbility
Putting it all together

As a reminder, the 12 steps for being a courageous leader take:

- ✔ Courage and commitment
- ✔ A willingness to step out of our comfort zone
- ✔ The need to readily adapt to change
- ✔ An obligation to develop our skill set and the skills within our organization

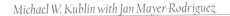

YOUR COURAGE MAY BE CHALLENGED!

Read the following statements and think about how you could add more value for your career, team, and organization.

Takes notes; where do you have opportunities to become a more courageous leader?

"A vision without a task is but a dream, a task without a dream is drudgery, a vision and a task is the hope of the world."--Church in Sussex, England c.1730

Passion is the catalyst for everything a leader does and it certainly removes the drudgery factor; your passion may be for an organization, a team, a department, or for you.

Do you know what you're passionate about?

Are you in the right job to leverage your passion?

$V, M, G + M = B^{TM}$

Vision, Mission, Goals and Measures = Behaviors

All your behaviors must link to what you say you are going to do.

You must be consistent in your hiring, reward, and performance appraisal processes, and your behaviors MUST link to your vision, mission, and goals.

__ALL BEHAVIORS MUST SUPPORT YOUR VISION, MISSION, and GOALS__

It's possible to get sidetracked by unclear priorities.

How many "urgent" issues have nothing to do with attaining your goals or supporting your vision and mission?

HIRE HARD OR BE READY TO MANAGE HARD

Which will better serve you?

Which could sabotage you?

We must have a selection process and remain disciplined with our defined criteria.

Don't hire on technical skills only or on soft-skill strengths similar to your own.

Be aware of your biases and use testing to assist with your hiring process.

A LEADER WHO UNDERSTANDS AND USES THE STRENGTHS OF SELF AND OTHERS OBTAINS OPTIMAL RESULTS

It's almost impossible to achieve your dream on your own. You need leadership, creativity, and a variety of strengths.

The best way for a leader to accomplish their dream is to let others participate in it.

Engage others that round out your style, step back, and let them soar.

Make the time and use appropriate resources to help others learn, grow and develop their strengths and reduce their weaknesses.

SUCCESS MEANS COMMUNICATING WITH OTHERS IN THEIR LANGUAGE

What level of communication do you prefer?

Do you want detailed reports or brief summaries?

You need to recognize your preferred style and have the skill to adapt it to the preferred style of your leader, business partners, and customers.

FEEDBACK IS THE CORNERSTONE FOR STRONG LEADERSHIP

Do you provide timely and meaningful feedback?

Are there times you resist giving feedback?

> Tip: Communicate how unproductive behaviors are impacting you and others; remain fact based and provide specific details.

GIVE AND RECEIVE FEEDBACK IN A HEALTHY, HONORING WAY

Is your intent to help others grow?

How receptive are you to what others recommend?

When on the receiving end, listen and take time to process what you heard instead of immediately reacting.

MANAGING CHANGE WITH A PURPOSE IS A RECIPE FOR CHAMPIONS

Recognize that it's human nature to resist change.

Communicate WHY change is necessary and what and who will be impacted.

If you're not in the position to share upcoming changes, don't deny that they may occur. Rather share that change is required for progress, and commit to communicating all changes when you are able to.

TRUE LEADERS UNDERSTAND THEIR THOUGHTS, FEELINGS, and BEHAVIORS

How can we learn from them?

What can they do for us?

The strongest leaders are conscious of how they think, feel, and act and appropriately adjust their styles based on situations and individuals.

Use your emotional intelligence to manage your actions and control your behaviors.

WHEN THINGS DON'T GO AS PLANNED, DON'T BEAT YOURSELF UP

Learn from it. Don't think in terms of good/bad, or right/wrong.

Consider what could be done differently to obtain the results you desire.

OVER-USING A STRENGTH MAY BECOME A WEAKNESS

Think in terms of "too much of a good thing". Let's say you love details and facts, and always want more. This could result in things never getting completed or the analysis/ paralysis syndrome.

What about being decisive? You may be quick to make decisions but could at times benefit from taking a bit more time for review and analysis.

Do you know what your strengths are? Do you take measures to ensure they don't become a weakness?

There is no right or wrong; there is the need to recognize when to use each approach.

LEADERSHIP IS A JOURNEY, NOT AN EVENT

We all want to become stronger leaders and know it is a process that occurs over time.

Progress can be made on a daily basis, but expect and plan for growth to continue through-out your career and your life.

Have a development plan and track your progress; this should include your strengths as well as your weaknesses.

COMMITMENT IS ALLOCATING TIME TO YOUR DIFFERING ROLES

LEADERSHIP = Inspiring and empowering others to go where they've never gone before and wouldn't go by themselves.

MANAGEMENT = Planning, Organizing, Controlling and following-up.

COACHING = Helping others achieve their desired goals and objectives.

TECHNICIAN = Doing the job or task extremely well.

Where do you spend most of your time? True leaders spend the least amount of their time in the role of technician.

WORK ON THE BUSINESS, NOT IN THE BUSINESS

As a leader, how much time do you spend on tactical issues?

Could delegation and strategizing be a better use of your time?

Assess the pulse of your organization, look to optimize processes, and don't forget to ask your team for their ideas and let them do what they do best.

RUN YOUR TEAM, DEPARTMENT, and ORGANIZATION LIKE A BUSINESS

You own it, lead it, and manage it.

Don't assess blame, be responsible and accountable.

Your behavior will inspire others to do the same.

COURAGEABILITY®

The ability to live both your dreams and professional life they way you want.

It's achieving your goals, ambitions and objectives.

We need the ability to activate it "on command".

Consider it a tool and trigger for strong leadership.

SELF ASSESSMENT

*Answer the following questions using a rating scale
of 1-8 (8 being a clear and consistent "yes")*

1. I have thought about what it is I want to do and accomplish in my life.
   1   2   3   4   5   6   7   8

2. I understand what a SMART goal is.
   1   2   3   4   5   6   7   8

3. I talk about my commitments to others.
   1   2   3   4   5   6   7   8

4. I understand others have unique strengths and talents.
   1   2   3   4   5   6   7   8

5. I know that communication is a key tool for leaders.
   1   2   3   4   5   6   7   8

6. I am comfortable with conflict and don't avoid it.
   1   2   3   4   5   6   7   8

7. One of my goals is to have others succeed.
   1   2   3   4   5   6   7   8

8. I know it's important to delegate to others.
   1   2   3   4   5   6   7   8

9. I understand the value of coaching and development
   1   2   3   4   5   6   7   8

10. I know the value of being calm and in control as a leader.
    1   2   3   4   5   6   7   8

11. Everything is not part of one's job and it is important to understand that.

    1   2   3   4   5   6   7   8

12. I understand the value of taking a chance.

    1   2   3   4   5   6   7   8

13. I am living my dream daily and helping others do the same.

    1   2   3   4   5   6   7   8

14. My goals are documented. I review them, and take action.

    1   2   3   4   5   6   7   8

15. I have commitments that are reviewed daily for action.

    1   2   3   4   5   6   7   8

16. I delegate assignments and use the talents of others.

    1   2   3   4   5   6   7   8

17. I regularly conduct one on one meetings with my team and others.

    1   2   3   4   5   6   7   8

18. I utilize my conflict skills all the time in approaching difficult situations.

    1   2   3   4   5   6   7   8

19. I work with others to succeed; if they move one step, I take a step with them.

    1   2   3   4   5   6   7   8

20. Business/results have grown because I have others performing tasks.

    1   2   3   4   5   6   7   8

21. My leadership skills are applied with my staff and customer interactions.

    1   2   3   4   5   6   7   8

22. I utilize emotional intelligence skills to deal with difficult situations.

    1   2   3   4   5   6   7   8

23. I reward and recognize accomplishments and provide feedback as a process.

    1   2   3   4   5   6   7   8

24. I fail and I succeed and debrief both with my staff.

    1   2   3   4   5   6   7   8

PLOT YOUR RESULTS

Directions:

1. Plot questions 1 – 12. These statements reflect the strength of your beliefs.
2. Plot questions 13 – 24. These statements assess how strongly your behaviors are used to "live" your beliefs.

CourageAbility™ Chart

Scoring your Beliefs and Behaviors

SCORE

Questions

	1	2	3	4	5	6	7	8
24								
23								
22								
21								
20								
19								
18								
17								
16								
15								
14								
13								
12								
11								
10								
9								
8								
7								
6								
5								
4								
3								
2								
1								

There were two types of questions that you answered. The odd numbered questions dealt with your beliefs and your feelings; the even numbered questions revolved around the actions and behaviors you engage in to support your beliefs.

Were any questions rated with a score lower than 5? Do questions 13 – 24 have lower scores than questions 1 – 12? These are your discovery areas. Take the time to review both your thoughts and actions to determine how they could be more aligned.

IT'S TIME TO MAKE A COMMITMENT!

» Select ONE leadership dimension you will change starting today.

That dimension is:

_____

What are you going to do differently?

_____

_____

_____

» Select TWO other dimensions that you will incorporate into your development plan.

They are:

_____

_____

Remember, courage and commitments are required for being a strong leader.

Leverage the fear and courage you feel to be even more inspired and effective!

Wishing you Success,
Mike and Jan

Michael Kublin
President PeopleTek Inc.
mkublin@peopletekcoaching.com
888.565.9555 ext. 711

Jan Mayer-Rodriguez
Vice President PeopleTek Inc.
jan@peopletekcoaching.com
888.565.9555 ext. 712

PeopleTek is dedicated to developing leaders, teams and organizations to be courageous in all their pursuits and endeavors.

Michael Kublin is the founder and President of PeopleTek, a leadership, development and coaching company created in 1996 for individuals, teams and organizations that have a need to transform their leadership skills and change their culture.

Mike developed The Leadership Journey and Team Leadership Journey programs which are multi session self reflective "people skill" programs that enable leaders and their organizations to be more effective and productive.

Participants and teams identify what holds them back and learn to improve their decision making skills and enhance their behaviors while strategically implementing internal and external business practices. These new behaviors and processes enable leaders to build stronger organizations by successfully attracting, hiring, and inspiring people to support one another and drive the bottom line.

Prior to PeopleTek, Mike worked in various leadership positions within Information Technology and Sales at American Express and Electronic Data Systems. Michael graduated with a Bachelor of Science degree in Business Administration from the University of Florida and received his Masters Degree in Business Administration from Nova Southeastern University.

Jan Mayer-Rodriguez is editor-in-chief for PeopleTek's weekly leadership tip, and assists with developing and enhancing business relationships with PeopleTek's customer base. She also monitors customer relations and identifies developmental opportunities for organizations and individuals.

Jan had a 27 year career with American Express with positions spanning Customer Relations, Client Support, Project Management, Quality Control, and Six Sigma. This multi faceted focus on leadership included improving internal/external customer and employee satisfaction levels, delivering superior products, and building effective cross team behaviors.

Born and raised in Michigan, Jan graduated from Eastern Michigan University with Bachelor of Science degrees in Criminal Justice and Sociology.